The 5x2 Method

Chris DiVecchio

DEDICATION

We know stress can cause physical harm as well as premature death, but the reality is that we can actually do something about it. Stress is undoubtedly an inevitable part of life, but just like anything else we face as human beings, there is cause and effect. It's how we allow the stress to affect us and what we do to shift the stress away from our minds and our bodies that can provide the freedom from pain and suffering.

My 5x2 Method has the ability to dramatically reduce stress and open your eyes to things that have been right in front of you hiding in plain sight. When stress starts interfering with your ability to live a normal life for an extended period, it becomes even more dangerous. The longer the stress lasts, the worse it is for both your mind and body. You might feel fatigued, unable to concentrate or irritable for no good reason. But chronic stress causes wear and tear on your body and can tend to make existing problems worse. Chronic stress can also cause disease and because of changes in your body, can lead to overeating, smoking, drinking and other bad habits people use as a coping mechanism.

The 5x2 Method is your opportunity to break free from those common patterns and choose a healthier approach that is both powerful and empowering. This book is dedicated to anyone who is struggling to find peace in their lives. Happiness is a conscious choice, not an automatic response. It is my hope that if you've found this book to have had a positive impact on your life, that you will share it with someone else who may benefit from it the same way you have. It could be a complete stranger whom you've just met or a close friend who is looking for solutions. We only get one chance at this life, and everyone deserves happiness.

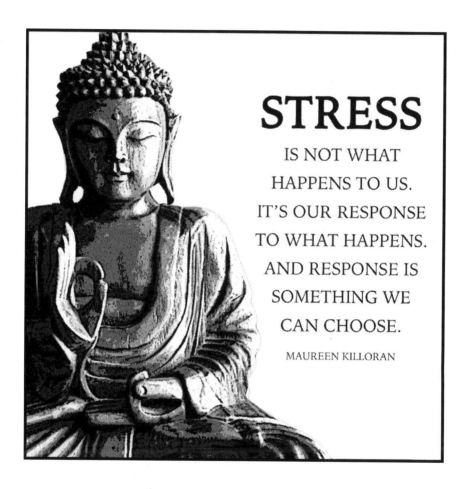

STRESS
IS NOT WHAT
HAPPENS TO US.
IT'S OUR RESPONSE
TO WHAT HAPPENS.
AND RESPONSE IS
SOMETHING WE
CAN CHOOSE.

MAUREEN KILLORAN

CONTENTS

ACKNOWLEDGMENTS

I'd like to thank my parents for all their love and support in pursuing my life of happiness. No matter what decisions I've made, they have backed me 100% and have always been in favor of my happiness first and foremost.

It has helped shape my life experiences which makes it possible for me to share this book with you.

I'd also like to thank Everyone who contributed to the development of this book. This has been 2 years in the making and would not be possible without a team of dedicated like-minded individuals.

Reconnecting with Elise Quevedo, my co-writer, was no accident. Thank you for really seeing me and helping me put my vision on paper to share with the world.

And last, but certainly not least, I want to give special thanks to my beautiful life partner and fiancé for pushing me to finish this book. Since the day she came into my life she has amplified all five of my senses to levels I never even knew were possible.

I can't wait to see what our next adventure is going to be. I love you!

Chapter 1

INTRODUCTION TO THE 5x2

Don't overthink it. Just begin.
-Rich Roll-

The alarm clock rang, I reached up for a long deep stretch, rolled out of bed, pulled on my slippers, walked downstairs to grind my coffee and breathe in the aromas, read through my morning inspiration from the Daily Om, turned on a Gary Vee Podcast, poured myself a cup of coffee and bingo.....it hit me!

The 5x2 was something that I had been performing every single morning without even consciously knowing it. I've always been very aware of my senses; however, now that I had this awakening, I started to connect happy, positive feelings with specific memories that were triggered by any one of the 5 senses. I like to think that my subconscious understood this concept long before I did and was in some way looking for a way to always keep me in a positive state of mind.

Now that I had been awakened to this new idea, I was surprised to discover that I had also been doing a version of The 5x2 at night before bed. I'd come home, light some candles and a stick of Nag Champa incense, turn on some nice ambient music, jump on my foam roller to loosen and stretch my body, drink a warm cup of "sleepy time tea", read a few pages of a book and then fall asleep listening to a podcast. In short, I was intentionally setting my subconscious to generate more positive thoughts and energy through the sleeping hours. Whether this was a placebo effect or not, I could tell that incorporating the 5x2 into two crucial points of my day, first thing when I wake up and last thing before I go to bed, was improving the quality of my life.

I decided to test The 5x2 with a few of my clients, and I found that just by simply explaining what I wanted them to do, their energy was shifting into a more positive state. Most clients I work with have issues with energy during the day or trouble sleeping at night. By Offering a simple concept that could easily be incorporated into their daily routine and potentially change the way they feel, gave them hope. Low and behold, they were getting better quality sleep, more energy during the day, sharper mental acuity at work, their responses to challenges were handled with much more patience and ease, and their social lives improved because of a more optimistic outlook on a daily basis.

So, who is this book for?

I see this as huge value to those who are already conscious and looking for a way to take it to the next level. By performing the 5x2 method before your mediation, you are expanding and opening up your level of awareness and creating a clean, healthy, positive environment for the meditative state to transcend to deeper levels.

The 5x2 Method is for people who may already be doing some sort of 5x2 but have no clue they are because they are not conscious. Once the 5x2 method is brought to your awareness, it changes the experience you have with it and enriches the experience of the positive feedback loop that it is intended to create.

For example, someone who wakes up in the morning and grinds their coffee may just grind their coffee, quickly throw it in the machine and then move on to the next task. That same person who reads The 5x2 will now grind their coffee and stop to take 2 seconds to smell the aroma of the beans before they pour it into the machine.

It is for people who are completely asleep and are in search of something that will open up some sort of spiritual awakening. Often times these people either have no clue where to begin looking for answers, or they think it's too complicated and time-consuming. Meditation is an overwhelming, scary word for them. These people need a quick solution that makes sense and can easily be integrated into their everyday life without much interruption.

Lastly, this book is also for people who struggle with managing stress. Reducing stress will help you be more productive and open your eyes to be able to see things more clearly. Self-doubt and stress cloud your ability to truly see and appreciate what's around you.

Less clouds = more clarity.

Stress management is all about taking charge of your lifestyle, thoughts, emotions, and the way you deal with problems. Learn to say "no", avoid people who stress you out and take control of your environment.

Chris DiVecchio

Chapter 2

THE POWER OF USING YOUR SENSES

The best results I have had in my life; the most enjoyable times,
have all come from asking the simple question:
"What is the worst that could happen?"
-Tim Ferris-

As human beings we are very fortunate to experience 5 powerful senses:

- The power of sight
- The power of smell
- The power of hearing/sound
- The power of taste
- The power of touch

It is these senses that allow us to experience the world we live in which is a very unique way and we will dissect all of them in the next chapters.

If you're lucky enough to have all 5 senses, then you're probably like most who take their senses for granted. Don't wait to lose any of them to appreciate what you have. Someone who may have lost their vision probably thinks about the times they wished they had looked into their loved one's eyes deeper. Or maybe you lost your hearing in an accident, and you wished you would have spent more time listening to the ocean.

Did you know you use at least one of your five senses every moment of the day, even when you are asleep?

Each sense has its own special power, but it is when they are used in combination that we create those unforgettable experiences. There is a reason as to why we reminisce about events from the past. We are drawn to those experiences that provide us with multi-sensory stimulation.

Think back to when you were a child for a moment, and you were at school. Was it noisy? Peaceful? What did the smell remind you of?
As an example, many studies have found that children attending schools under the flight paths of large airports lag behind in their exam results.

Bridget Shield, a professor of acoustics, says, "Everything points to a detrimental impact of the noise on children's performance, in numeracy, in literacy, and in spelling."

When it comes to smell, do you know many schools now use scents in classrooms to help with cognitive performance? From grapefruit scent for math to lavender for French and spearmint for history.

Back in 2003, Psychologist Mark Moss carried out cognitive tests on subjects who were exposed to either lavender or rosemary aromas. He said, "Rosemary, in particular, caught my attention as it is considered to be arousing and linked to memory, whereas lavender is considered to be sedating."

Moss found those who were smelling lavender performed significantly worse in working memory tests and had impaired reaction times for both memory and attention-based tasks.

When it comes to colors, think back to the days you would sit at the dinner table, and refused to eat something because you did not like the look, smell or feel of it when touched. Senses have been a part of us for so long that we don't see the importance of the big part they play in our lives.

Close your eyes for a moment and think of a story, an experience you've had where two or more senses took part.

I can think of a movie theatre. Think of the last 3D movie you watched. Not only does our sight come into play, but when you combine it with the surround sound, your movie experience gets heightened. It makes you feel like you are inside the movie. And how about the soundtrack? Our minds associate the way music makes us feel, to the memories of when we first heard it or what was happening at the time.

I can think of a luxury bed in a 5-star hotel. The scent they put on the pillows, the feel of the luxury linen. There are many hotel chains known for that comfort, and they play on that. They know how important it is to make guests feel the comfort as if they were in their own home. They want their guests to come back, so they make sure you associate your night sleep with a night at home.

I would love to hear some of the stories that came to your mind.

Just like humans, animals were created with five senses, and although they use theirs in different ways, I believe we can use a few examples from their behavior to see the power of what we can do.

As we know, the five senses are controlled by five organs: The eyes, nose, tongue, ears, and skin. In animals, some of these senses are used more than others, just like a human who may not have all five senses.

Here is a list of a few animals that are known for using their power for survival.

The Eagle

Did you know they can see about eight times as far as humans can? Eagles can also quickly shift focus, allowing them to essentially "zoom" in on their prey. They also can see a wider range of colors than we can, allowing them to differentiate small changes in coloration in their prey.

The Bear

This is an interesting one. If you happen across a bear when camping, the first instinct would be to run or sneak away quietly so they wouldn't see or hear you. Instinctually, this makes sense because we think of bears as powerful and dangerous animals.

Considering they can weigh up to 1500 lbs and reach nearly 10ft in height, it is just logical to fear and respect them. However, what you might not know is that the bear does not have the greatest sight or hearing. What they do have is one of the best sense of smell. It is how they locate food and also how they signal each other.

The Moth

Want to know why it is sometimes hard to catch a moth? Because they have been named as having some of the best hearing in the world! They are able to hear a higher frequency than bats which are among the top 10 animals with the best hearing.

The Catfish

This may be unusual, but did you know that a catfish can detect earthquakes days in advance? Unlike any other fish, they don't have scales all over their body. They have very soft skin allowing them a greater sense of touch. And not only touch, but they also have some of the best sense of taste too.

The average human has 10,000 taste buds, and this fish can have up to 175,000. That says it all.

With all of this in mind, can you understand a bit more how each sense is used? Let's break them down.

Chapter 3

SIGHT
-THE EYES ARE THE WINDOW TO THE SOUL-

I know nothing with any certainty, but the sight of the stars makes
me dream.
-Vincent Van Gogh-

Fact: The surface of the earth curves out of sight at around five
kilometers. Did you know human vision can see far beyond that?

And when we talk about sight and vision, we can take it to the next
level and say that the Power of Sight will lead you to the Opening of
consciousness. I recommend reading "The Flames of Alertness:
Discover the Power of Consciousness!" By Frank M. Wanderer,
which you will also enjoy.

Today I focus on what we can see. It is one of the first senses we use
in the morning as we wake up and open our eyes.

Be grateful each day for this power that not everyone can enjoy.
From the smile of a loved one next to you to a beautiful sunrise.

Take a moment to think about the first things you see when you get
up in the morning. Are you smiling? You should. What we first see
kicks off our mood.

I work in a field where sight is extremely important. Although I instill in my clients that mind and body are connected, we need to look both at the physical and mind state of a person for health. When you look in the mirror, the first thing you see is how you look on the outside. When was the last time you looked in the mirror and truly looked at who you are with the power of sight?

Within the personal development world and teachings, we learn to look and focus beyond what everyone else sees.

We tend to be the worst critics of ourselves so let's do an exercise together. Find a mirror, look at yourself and find 3 things you like about yourself.

For this, you need to take a couple of minutes, smile and truly look. Is it your eyes, the way you smile, the way you stand tall, what you are wearing at this instant since you chose those garments?

How did that feel? We live in such a hectic, fast pacing world that we don't always get a chance to truly look at ourselves.

How about the people close to your circle? What attracts you to them when you see them? Is it their warm smile when you say hello, the way you see them behave with other people, their reaction to one of your jokes, or how they pay attention to people when they talk?

Every day we talk to people. We can stop for a few seconds and reflect on what we observe. How about you do that tomorrow and send me some stories?

With the saying "the eyes are the window to the soul," we often think about observing what's going on with other people when we look at them or allowing other people to get a glimpse of what's really going on inside of ourselves. However, another interesting perspective is to open up your windows to let something in to feed your soul. Just like you would open up a window to catch a breeze or hear the sound of a bird chirping.

I use my sense of sight most powerfully when I'm reading quotes. Quotes are often experiences that people have put into their own form of expression. When I read a quote, it opens my mind to consider the possibility of that perspective. At times, it may challenge my own beliefs, and in other moments it may awaken beliefs that I have forgotten about. Either way, I choose to start my morning 5x2 by reading an entry from The Daily Om, which is a platform developed by Madison Taylor and Scott Blum to offer messages of consciousness and awareness to people from all walks of life. They take a universal approach to holistic living for the mind, body, and spirit that supports people who want to live a conscious lifestyle. I have certainly found it to be powerful in my life. Maybe you will too.

People are just one of the focuses of our daily lives. How about when we travel or go for a walk by ourselves in the forest. What do you see? Because we are less distracted by the sound of others or things, we can focus more on what we come across.

Only our imagination sees the way the tree leaves sway, the way the sun shines and reflects on the water of a lake, the way a plane flies up high in the sky, the way the clouds move and form shapes.

Did you know the eyes provide a lot of information about someone else's emotional state? When we are sad, our eyes look smaller, when we are happy we tend to open our eyes wider making them look brighter, which is why we often call them "bright eyes" when you come across a happy person.

Want to truly know if someone is smiling for real or faking it? Then look at their eyes. A smile by our mouth can be easily faked, but the way our eyes react cannot.

Earlier I mentioned bears. If you were to come across one while on a walk, your eye pupils would dilate in reaction to what you see.

When we say, "the eyes are the window to the soul," it's because there is a lot to be said based on how our pupils react which it cannot control.

Psychologists (1) consider pupil dilation to be an honest cue to sexual or social interest. They consider pupil size in terms of the two functions of vision—exploration and exploitation. When we're exploring our environments, we're on the lookout for threats and opportunities, so we're in a heightened state of arousal. Visual sensitivity is most important in exploration, so our pupils are wide open, taking in as much visual information as possible.

Once we've identified an object of interest and have it under our control, we shift to exploitation mode: We need to examine the item carefully to find all the ways we can use it and to understand it as fully as possible. Visual acuity is most important, and our pupils dilate or contract so that just the right amount of light comes in.

The so-called pupillary light response isn't just a mechanical reaction to the amount of ambient light, as is the aperture on a camera. Instead, the pupils also adjust according to our emotions and expectations. Thus, the eyes may be the windows to the soul, but the pupils tell a lot about what's going on in the mind of another person.

Let's go beyond what we can physically see and talk about the power of seeing something and how it shifts you. We talk about visualization.

Mental practice, positive mental attitude can get you closer to your goals, to where you want to be in life. There have been many studies looking at brain patterns, where research has revealed that mental practices are almost as effective as actual physical practice.

For instance, in his study on everyday people, Guang Yue, an exercise psychologist from Cleveland Clinic Foundation in Ohio, compared "people who went to the gym with people who carried out virtual workouts in their heads." He found a 30% muscle increase in the group who went to the gym. However, the group of participants who conducted mental exercises of the weight training increased muscle strength by almost half as much (13.5%). This average remained for 3 months following the mental training.

Many athletes use this technique to mentally prepare as they visualize their journey to the win. They go through self-confirmation and affirmations. So why not apply that to ourselves in our daily lives?

Combining what we see with our eyes and what we see in our minds creates a powerful combination.

Chapter 4

SMELL
-STOP AND SMELL THE ROSES-

Scent is our most primitive sense, it's the closest thing to the
emotional brain. It penetrates you.
You love it, and you want to be part of it.
-Isabelle Ramsay-Brackstone-

Fact: Did you know people can detect at least one trillion distinct
scents? Less than 100 years ago, scientists thought we could only
detect 10,000 different smells. Now with all the technology and
different research tests, those results have significantly increased,
showing us how powerful our noses can be.

So, how does this sense actually work since we all use it every single
day? Amber Luong, MD, PhD, Assistant Professor at the University
of Texas says:

"When odors enter the nose, they travel to the top of the nasal cavity
to the olfactory cleft where the nerves for smell are located. There,
the odorant is detected by various receptors located on the nerve
cells, and the combination of activated nerves travel to the brain. The
combination of activated nerves generates all the unique smells that
we as humans can detect."

There is so much more to the power of smell than we think, so I want to share with you a few facts that will make you look at this sense with different eyes.

According to a 2012 study published in the journal of Psychological Science, we can smell fear and disgust through sweat, which then leads to experiencing the same emotions.

Researchers collected sweat from men as they watched movies that caused these feelings of fear and disgust. To remain odor-neutral for the sweat test, the men used scent-free products, and quit smoking and alcohol. Women participants then completed visual search tests, while unknowingly smelling the sweaty samples. The women's eye movements and facial expressions were recorded during this time.

The researchers found that women who smelled the "fear sweat" opened their eyes widely in a fearful expression, and women who smelled the "disgust sweat" also displayed facial expressions of disgust.

Although there is no database for human scent yet, did you also know just like a fingerprint, every human has their own distinct odor? When we look at what each sense can do, it is like entering into a new world we didn't know anything about.

Next to sight, smell is the most important sense we have. 75% of the emotions we create each day are affected by smell.

So, what does "stop & smell the roses" mean? In a nutshell: Don't be too busy in life, take a timeout, take time to notice the things and people around you. Simply, slow down!

This expression is more than just about smelling a rose, which always opens our sensory buds. It is about how to live our life, and this is what The 5x2 Method is all about. It is about reflecting on the little things we do on a daily basis.

Smelling the roses can be applied to areas such as making time for family and friends, building deeper relationships, and appreciating the small things.

For example, how about having dinner on the table instead of in front of the TV? Make time to go sightseeing, make time to call friends or family that you have not spoken to in a while.

It all comes down to planning. Get your calendar out and mark important dates and times just like you would for work schedules. Spending time with friends and family is good for your overall physical and mental health.

When was the last time you truly listened to the people you are surrounded with? With the distractions of technology, we need to re-learn to be more present. That means putting away your cellphone and engaging with people the old-fashioned way.

Being present, in the moment, appreciating the small things is all just practice, like anything else in life. We can start with a few seconds at a time, then build up to a few minutes a day. When was the last time you went for a walk in the park and were able to focus on the smells around you? The smell of fresh pine trees, the smell of the earth after it's been raining, Nature says, "look at me, I'm here."

There are just certain smells that have the ability to instantly put a smile on your soul, let alone your face. For me, that's fresh ground coffee beans. That's not to say that there aren't several other smells that can shift me in an instant, I just like the smell of fresh ground coffee beans as the motivating smell to start my day.

Before I became aware of the power of The 5x2, I used to just grind my beans and pour them into the coffee machine and not think twice about it. Now, every morning I head downstairs with my slippers on my feet, grind my beans, take a slow deep inhale of the aroma that immediately reminds me of the simple pleasures in life.

One quote that comes to mind every single time is "remember to stop and smell the roses." Except in this case, it's coffee!

Chapter 5

SOUND
-MUSIC TO YOUR EARS-

Listen to the wind, it talks. Listen to the silence, it speaks. Listen to your heart, it knows.
-Native American Proverb-

Fact: Hearing is the ability to perceive sound by detecting vibrations, changes in the pressure of the surrounding medium through time, through an organ such as the ear.

This is another sense which is used 24 hours a day and the most efficient and sensitive sensory organ.

Because the way we look at the world is strongly influenced by the power of eyesight, we don't always understand the big part this sense plays.

Here is why we should pay more attention (2):

Hair Cells

The inner ear contains about 3,000 inner and 12,000 outer hair cells. They are extremely sensitive and can be destroyed by noise, causing irreparable hearing loss.

Health

People with untreated hearing loss often feel isolated from others and suffer more from depression and insomnia.

Recognize Emotions

We can tell the mood of people, just by hearing the intonation of their voice.

Warning System

Our hearing is on alert 24 hours a day, even when we are sleep.

Distinction

Our ears can distinguish up to 400,000 different sounds. They process twice as many impressions as our eyes.

First Hearing Experiences

Babies can hear from about 16 weeks after conception. After birth, they immediately recognize their mother by her voice.

Now that we have a few facts and a better understanding of how hearing works, let's talk about "Music to your ears."

This saying means "something that is very pleasant or gratifying to hear." Just like when I first came up with The 5x2 Method, and I was listening to a Gary Vee Podcast, I aim to show you that everything you do and hear affects your wellbeing.

What is your go-to playlist when working out? What do you listen to when turning on the radio in the car? Who do you call to have a good conversation?

As you get more in tune with this method and learn to quickly identify your 5, it will all make more sense.

What you hear is attached to the way you feel. Hear something negative, it will put you in a negative state of mind. Hear something positive, and it will put you in a positive state of mind.

The Law Of Attraction teaches us the Universe can only understand two vibrations, negative and positive. I believe it is exactly the same with the power of hearing.

Close your eyes and think of the last conversation you had or the last thing you were listening to. What was it? How did it make you feel? Did it have a positive or negative vibe?

All our senses are connected with the way our mind and thinking react, and even though we may focus on one, they all have a domino effect. Say you are talking to a loved one, and you hear something you don't agree with. This triggers a feeling inside which makes the brain react in multiple ways. And vice versa, if you hear something you agree with that makes you smile, endorphins are released making you feel happy. It is all connected.

Everything around us vibrates, we are surrounded by sound all the time.

I recently read an experiment by Doctor Masaru Emoto, which I have to share it with you.

Dr. Emoto, a graduate of the Yokohama Municipal University's Department of Humanities and Sciences, and author of the bestselling book *Messages from Water*, gained worldwide acclaim for his groundbreaking research and his discovery that water is affected by vibrational sound in some very surprising ways.

In his experiments, Dr. Emoto analyzed the formation of differently shaped crystals in water as it was exposed to different sounds in different forms. Part of his research included verbal affirmations, thoughts, music, and even prayers from a priest. He focused on verbal affirmations of love and gratitude as they were being directed toward water that was sitting in a Petri dish. He then analyzed the water under a microscope and took before and after pictures to document the change.

Dr. Emoto and his team observed that after the experiment very beautiful crystals had formed in some of the frozen water samples where the positive vibrational waves were directed. Dr. Emoto then exposed water samples to music from Mozart, Beethoven, and other classical composers and found that beautiful crystal shapes also formed in these samples. He also experimented with people saying things like "you fool," "I will kill you," and other unpleasant phrases using a harsh tone. Dr. Emoto found that ugly, incomplete, and malformed crystals were formed in the water samples exposed to these negative expressions and tones.

Dr. Emoto concluded that any sound is vibration, and vibrations such as music and other positive sounds including the human voice can be a form of healing energy. His research also showed that thoughts emit vibrations at frequencies we can't yet precisely determine, and that they too have the power to heal.

Another example is classical music and how it can help students get the most out of their revision time when prepping for exams. There is a reason we choose more upbeat music for a workout and a more relaxed tone when on a cool-down or simply wanting to relax.

There was research carried out by academics in the US and France which found that listening to classical music while studying can actually help students score higher in their assessments.

Classical music can help both calm students down and make them more receptive to new information.

Classic FM presenter, Bill Turnbull, said:

"Last year, thousands of students tuned into Classic FM to help them get through the busy revision and exam period so, this year, we have created a list of the most relaxing, inspirational, and motivational pieces to help them keep their eyes on the ball."

So, to help you out, I will re-share his list of top ten classical tracks:

10.　　Piano Concerto No. 23 – Wolfgang Amadeus Mozart

9.　　The Hours – Philip Glass

8.　　Gymnopedie No. 1 – Erik Satie

7.　　Clair De Lune – Claude Debussy

6.　　Etudes – Claude Debussy

5.　　Academic Festival Overture – Johannes Brahms

4.　　Well-Tempered Clavier – Johann Sebastian Bach

3.　　A Beautiful Mind – James Horner

2.　　Goldberg Variations - Johann Sebastian Bach

1.　　Canon in D – Johann Pachelbel

As a Premier, Mind and Body trainer, I teach my clients about meditation and getting to know yourself. The sounds you hear can make a big difference to a successful meditation session and the ability to reach a new state of mind.

As I've been doing with the other senses, here is an experience I want to share about hearing.

I once read that a great listener is someone who makes the other person feel heard, not just someone who sits there quietly listening. The ears can be just as powerful if not more than the eyes. Do you ever notice that when people are deeply entrenched in a song, they close their eyes and let their ears do the seeing? How about when you make a wish? You close your eyes and listen to your own thoughts as you loft your deepest desire to whatever it is you hope to come true. Closing your eyes and allowing your ears to do what they do best can be incredibly powerful. I use sound in so many ways to shift me.

There are almost too many examples I could use here. I could literally write a whole book on this topic alone, but I will share the most common use of sound that I choose.

From the moment I wake up at 5:30am, I dedicate myself to my clients. It takes a tremendous amount of energy, mentally, physically, and emotionally. At times, I am left completely drained at the end of my day. It's crucial that I find a way to decompress and relax my mind and body. I was driving home from work one night and decided to put on my Coachella playlist. It was a mix of Thievery Corporation, Reggae, Chvrches, and The XX.

The music choice is objective and irrelevant because different types of music move people differently. However, the fact that it was my Coachella playlist is incredibly important and relevant because Coachella is one of my favorite music festivals, one that I've been going to for 8 years in a row, and has filled me with endless happy memories.

By simply hitting that playlist after a long day of work, I'm put into an instant state of bliss. I literally feel as though I'm back in the desert with the sun setting behind the mountains, a warm breeze blowing through the valley and the music echoing from one stage to the other.

Even as I write this memory, I feel myself take a deep breath and release the excitement that builds up from the memory that the music is responsible for. I encourage you to create a playlist of songs that remind you of happy memories and use that list intentionally. Start your day off with a song that gets you excited about life or when your super stressed out, dig into the playlist for a song that can calm you down and shift you into a happier state of mind.

Chapter 6

TASTE
-TASTE THE RAINBOW-

One cannot think well, love well, sleep well, if one has not dined
well.
-Virginia Woolf-

Fact: Did you know, the average person has up to 10,000 taste buds
and they are replaced every 2 weeks?

What did you taste last? Was it sweet, sour, salty, bitter or savory?
The sense of taste tends to be attached to the sense of smell. When
we don't know what someone is offering us, our first instinct is to
smell it, then our sensory system tells us if we might like it or not.
Both are chemical reactions that send messages to the brain

There is a very powerful link between what we taste and our
emotions. In the early days, taste aided us to identify food. It was
survival. A bitter or sour taste might indicate food was inedible and
the taste of sweet and salty was often a sign of good food. To this
day, we use a combination of these two senses to warn us away from
foods that may be dangerous.

As you delve into the practice of The 5x2 Method, I want you to take
time to enjoy what you taste. Let's take that cup of Joe in the
morning or tea (whichever you prefer), what is it about that drink in
particular that you enjoy?

Professor David Hill of the University of Virginia operates one of only a handful of laboratories worldwide studying the development of the taste system.

He said: "If I had to lose any of my five senses, I would choose to lose the taste sense, I need to be able to see and hear, to smell and feel, but I could do without my sense of taste if I had to. But as a neuroscientist, I've chosen to study taste because we actually know very little about it compared to those other senses. We can learn a great deal about all the senses and the development of the nervous system by studying the many interesting facets of taste because of some unique biological processes."

Using mice as models, Hill is looking at how huge changes can occur in neurodevelopment in the womb, depending on the diet of the mother during pregnancy. The taste system provides clues as to how the brain must continually process new information from new cells, and how modifications can ultimately become locked in once development slows and eventually stops in adulthood.

"One of our questions is, 'If taste cells are constantly turning over, how does the nervous system keep reliable information coming to the brain when the reception system is always changing?' We want to understand how the wiring changes in early development and adulthood," Hill said.

His findings demonstrate the importance of diet during pre-natal development. He has shown that the taste system is highly malleable, and taste preferences and aversions can be modified before birth, just as preferences can change throughout life based on changing diets.

"The central circuits that drive taste apparently have a great deal of plasticity," Hill said, meaning early diets, including the mother's diet while pregnant, could have a significant effect on the future dietary choices of offspring.

The world of taste can be quite fascinating, and we all have our preferences. There is so much expression in taste whether it be a home cooked meal or a glass of wine from your favorite Vineyard. A lot of pride is taken in sharing experiences through taste. The expression "made with love" is a real thing.

Sometimes you can actually taste the love. It's designed to elicit a specific response. Take one bite of your favorite meal or a sip of your favorite drink and instantly a memory is created. But just as easily as an incredible memory can be formed through taste, so can a bad memory. However, with The 5x2 Method, we only choose to focus on the positives.

With that said, I'll share my morning choice for taste. Remember, there is no right or wrong way to perform The 5x2. It's all about finding a list of 5 that weave seamlessly into your day as if it were as easy as taking a breath. Grinding my coffee beans and smelling the aroma is an incredible experience in itself, but a very close second is drinking my cup of coffee. I've learned a lot about coffee over the years and how to identify types of flavor profiles.

Although not as complex, it's much like wine in the sense that different regions have distinct flavors. There's front end and back end flavors, and a very specific intensive harvesting process that the beans go through to maintain the integrity of the taste. These are the thoughts that drift through my mind as I sip my coffee, with an appreciation for what it took to deliver that experience.

After the first few sips go down the hatch, I'm almost instantly put on a beach in Hawaii where I've enjoyed some of my favorite cups of Kona coffee.

I challenge you to explore what it is that you appreciate so much about a particular taste you find so appealing. You may end up finding it at the top of your own 5x2 list.

Chapter 7

TOUCH
-TOUCH HAS A MEMORY-

Touch comes before sight, before speech. It is the first language
and the last, and it always tells the truth.
-Margaret Atwood-

Fact: The somatosensory system is a part of the nervous system. This
is a complex system of sensory neurons and pathways that respond
to changes at the surface or inside the body. Touch is the act you
perform when you hold, caress or feel something.

As we get older, our sense of touch gets worse, which is why we need
to enjoy everything we do in life and why practicing The 5x2 Method
each day will help you experience the senses to their full potential.

I mentioned how, when I came up with this concept, my experience
at the time was the feeling of my feet in my slippers. Every day, we
put clothes on, we touch someone in the arm, we feel the breeze
across our face, the heat of the water in the shower…

Stop for a second and think of the last thing you felt against your
skin. Was it good? Bad? We have a complex system that can be both
pleasurable and painful. The caress of someone close to us can give
us pleasure, and the thorn of a rose can be painful when touched by
mistake.

It was John Keats who said, "Touch has a memory." Let's reflect on that.

Take the touch of a stranger versus the touch of a loved one. It is not the same to have a pat on the back from a colleague when they congratulate you than a loved one who puts their hand on your back, and you feel that meaningful touch you have felt before. Our bodies can remember a good meaningful touch, especially because it is also combined with the power of sight. We see the person who is touching us.

Take babies as an example. A baby senses and feels when a stranger gives them a hug, there is no bond there. But when their mom, dad or someone close to them gives them a hug, they recognize the person, they see them, they have a memory of who is making that touch feel more special.

Touch allows us to have multi-sensory experiences in different situations. It is why education is so important from a young age when it comes to experiencing what we can feel when we touch things or people.

Babies and small children are fascinated with bubbles, squishy things, pretty much anything they have not experienced as yet.

Being comfortable is something that we all crave. Often times I've found myself running through my life so busy that I forget to check in with how I'm feeling. I don't mean how I'm feeling mentally and emotionally, I mean physically. The body has an insane ability to adapt to pain, so if something is causing hurt, it will adjust its sensors so you can learn to tolerate it.

It's not until we are out of that discomfort that we then realize how uncomfortable we really were. It was only a few years ago that I became insanely aware of my feet. We are on our feet the majority of our lives, so it makes sense that we carry a lot of stress and tension in that particular area of our body. I now spend an incredible amount of time and energy dedicated to showing my feet some love. Between getting foot massages regularly and doing my own deep tissue manipulation at home, my feet have never felt better. Starting my day off with the touch portion of my 5x2 honoring my feet with my favorite pair of slippers is my reminder to keep showing them love.

As we grow older, we are so used to our surroundings that we don't pay attention to this sense unless it is to avert danger.

So, let's take a moment together and look around. Where are you right now? What can you touch? Feel? Are you at home with a smooth, cozy blanket that makes you feel warm? What are you wearing? How do your shoes feel? What about your clothes? How does your skin feel when you put them on?

A while back I read an article by Imogen Lamport about how your clothes make you feel. She mentioned how garments can make you feel both more alive and vibrant or dull and lifeless.

We talk about the importance of the human touch, and clothes are equally as important for your own self-belief system.

As Imogen said:

"If you want your clothes to make you feel more powerful at work, consider adding more yang elements to your outfits such as:

1. Structured garments like jackets,

2. Straighter vertical lines,

3. Fabric that has some weight and substance,

4. Darker colors paired with lighter colors to create more contrast, which will make you appear more authoritative.

Your exercise clothes should also make you feel strong. Saggy baggy old outside tee shirts won't give you this power. You want your exercise clothes to make you feel confident and powerful which will assist you in your exercise regime.

Even the type of material and colors you are wearing can change the mood you are in. From lighter clothing to feel more relaxed to heavier clothing to feel stronger.

Why is it that we also feel better after shower/bath? Not only does it feel good against our skin, but it is also full of both physical and psychological health benefits.

As a trainer, I help my clients by educating them on how to have a good workout and work on their mindset and wellbeing. Now with the help of The 5x2 Method, everyone will have access to a template that you can take with you everywhere you go.

Touch is the first language we all learn no matter where we are born, but that sometimes we take for granted. It can also be a cultural thing as to how we experience touch with others. Where in some countries warm hug embraces are your basic hello, creating a more immediate bond with a stranger versus others where just a hard handshake is exchanged.

As you can see, all senses have receptors that when combined they can create a magical experience which make you feel at ease. That, in a nutshell, is what I want everyone to do. To pay close attention to what is around you and use The 5x2 Method to make life more meaningful.

Chapter 8

THE LAW OF COMPOUNDING FACTORS

Find something you're passionate about and keep tremendously
interested in it.
-Julia Child-

One of the things I base my programs on is preventative health and
wellness.

I'm all for being proactive and trying to mitigate any controllable
health issues. The way I approach this is not with a quick fix trendy
concept. It's actually quite the contrary. I use a strategic process that
requires something that most of us struggle with, patience. I call it
stacking pennies.

The penny is very interesting. It's a single item that is viewed in
multiple ways. Some would see a penny on the ground and not even
think twice about picking it up because it's "just a penny." Another
person might walk by that penny, pick it up and put it in their pocket.
Now, the truth about that situation is, that neither person in that
scenario experienced anything different in their lives based on the
choice they made. The person who walked by the penny went on
with their day just fine, as well as the person who picked it up and
put in their pocket.

However, if that same situation played out exactly the same way every
day for 1 year, the individual outcomes would certainly be different

by the end of the year. The person who picked up one penny every day would have a stack of pennies and the person who couldn't care less about the penny would have nothing. The moral of this story is that sometimes the little mundane things that seem like they bring no value, turn out to be the biggest that we could ever imagine over time. Hence, The Law of Compounding Factors.

Just like the penny, we can apply that same model to anything we do in our lives and watch it multiply. It's only a matter of deciding what you want to grow. Unfortunately, most people are unconsciously floating through each day, so they end up compounding the wrong areas of their lives until they find themselves at rock bottom. Someone who is unconscious and unhappy may choose to have a few drinks after work to calm the stress. A couple of drinks that night won't make a difference one way or another. However, a couple of drinks a night, 7 nights a week, every month for an entire year may cause some problems. That same person could very easily choose to replace those drinks every night with the treadmill as a way to manage their stress and what do you think the difference in those choices would be? Dramatically different.

You see, the idea of The 5x2 Method is to bring the power of your five senses to your consciousness so you can apply The Law of Compounding Factors and watch your mind simply shift into a consistent state of optimism. It's literally like pouring gasoline on a fire. This, in turn, will ideally help develop a better pattern of decision making that you watch compound over time leading you down the path of happiness. Learning how to harness the power of your senses and use them deliberately to fuel your mind, body, and spirit is a skill that can easily be mastered. It just takes patience and consistency.

We all have a current state of thinking, acting, being, and doing that has been conditioned by our past. From our past childhood experiences to any relationship we've ever had, our minds have developed conditioned reactions and responses that contribute to the outcome of any decision we make. That's why it's incredibly important and effective to develop a high level of self-awareness if you want to have more of a positive impact on your results. What most people forget is that YOU get to decide how your day-to-day life plays out.

When learning how to apply The Law of Compounding Factors to The 5x2 Method, it's helpful to make notes of experiences that have had a positive impact in your life. Places you've seen, things you've done, people you've met, experiences you've had; really take a moment and playback the highlight reel of your life from as far back as you can remember. What's that one smell that could take you back to that one place you'll never forget? What's that one sound that vibrates through your soul every time you hear it? The power of those moments that we've experienced through each individual sense is buried deep within us, but if brought to the surface can shift us in an instance.

My goal is to have every person who picks up this book realize just how easy it is to change your life with conscious behavior consistently over time. I promise that if you apply The 5x2 Method every day, within a month, you will see a notable difference in how you view YOUR world. I've used this method with many of my clients from 12-68 years of age. The 5x2 Method does not discriminate nor does it have a right or wrong way to do it. It's whatever works best for you. Watch your relationships improve, sleep more deeply, wake up with more energy, open your mind to new ways of thinking, have deeper more meaningful conversations, listen more closely to things you may have never heard, try different foods that you've never dared to try, travel and explore new places that you've never even heard of.

These are all possible outcomes if you apply The Law of Compounding Factors to The 5x2 Method. The benefits stretch way beyond the immediate results. It begins to expand your life in a way you could never even imagine simply by tapping into your internal resources that we often undervalue.

Chapter 9

HOW TO DESIGN YOUR OWN 5x2

Almost everything will work again if you unplug it for a few
minutes . . . including you.
-Anne Lamott-

Remember, each sense has its own power. But combined, the power
can be overwhelming. And we are going for that overwhelming
power of happiness with this Method.

Don't Overthink It

Your 5x2 shouldn't be a chore or a struggle. It should be a simple
way to make some time for yourself every morning and night. In fact,
you may incorporate elements of a 5x2 into your day right now and
not even realize it. If you do, this journal will help you recognize
them and then create a purpose and intention behind them.

Start by thinking about what you're already doing in the mornings
and in the evenings. Do you drink a cup of coffee every morning
before you go to work? Maybe you put on a playlist in the morning
that gets your energy up. Those are a part of your 5x2.

Your 5x2 doesn't need to be what you're already doing. Maybe you're
always saying, "I'd love to have enough time to read before I go to
sleep." This is your chance to add something new to your routine.

It Can Change

Your 5x2 doesn't have to stay the same forever. If your routine isn't bringing you joy anymore, try to figure out what part has gotten old and change that. For example, maybe it's summer, and that warm cup of coffee or tea needs to be switched out for an iced one. Simply swapping out the feel of a warm cup for a cold one changes your sense of touch for your 5x2.

What's the Goal?

The end goal is for you to no longer need this book. It may seem weird to say that, but once you've tracked your 5x2 long enough in the journal, you will have reached the point where it becomes a conscious part of your daily routine. If you haven't used all the pages, share some with friends to help them get started

TIPS

Try using a particular scent more than once per day. For example, add lavender oil to a humidifier at morning and at night

Think about a song that brings you joy. Listen to that song in the morning. Similarly, if you have a song that calms you down, try listening to that song at night.

Print out your favorite quote and put it somewhere that you can look at it in the morning.

Search for a podcast that you find interesting. Listen to it in the morning or at night.

Try meditating for five minutes. There are many ways you can meditate, but the simplest one involves sitting down, closing your eyes and focusing on breathing in and breathing out.

Make your bed in the morning. Smoothing out your sheets doesn't just engage your senses, it also gives you a sense of accomplishment first thing in the morning (Tim Ferriss).

FORGETTING

If you realize halfway through the day that you forgot to write in your journal in the morning, you can still fill it out. Just take a few moments when you have time in the day to either do your morning 5x2 you had planned or another one that may fit your schedule.

For example, if you are at work, take a quick break, go outside and listen to your favorite song for a few minutes. It'll help you reset and remember to take time for yourself the rest of the day.

If you remember the next morning that you forget to do The 5x2 the previous night, use the "Something more" section of your previous page to reflect on why you didn't do it. Did you not want to? Were you too tired? Write it down to help hold yourself accountable.

SOMETHING MORE

The "Something more" section isn't just for when you forget to write your journal. You can also use it to write something good that happened that day. Maybe you had friends in town visiting, or you are out of town on business. Write that down to remember what you were doing and why your 5x2 may have changed from normal.

Chapter 10

THE 5x2 WORKOUT

It is time to put into action The 5x2 Method. Here are some examples of how it should look when you're ready to start.

The morning 5x2 has the 5 senses along with a goal for the day.

The nighttime 5x2 has the 5 senses along with something you're grateful for that day and a "something more" option if you wanted to add any other notes.

<u>Here is a morning 5x2 sample</u>

Say your morning routine involves drinking a cup of coffee and watching "The Today Show" in your favorite pair of slippers. Here's what your morning 5x2 would look like:

SAMPLE 1

This morning

I saw…The Today Show

I heard…a new band

I smelled…coffee

I tasted…coffee

I felt…my slippers

Today's goal is to…go for a 30-minute walk at work

The nighttime 5x2

Now for the night portion, maybe you like to read a book before bed. Instead of reading it right before you go to sleep, try starting an hour before with a glass of wine and some music in the background.

Sample

Tonight

I saw…Harry Potter and the Prisoner of Azkaban

I heard…jazz music

I smelled…my red wine

I tasted… my wine

I felt…my blanket

I am grateful for…a delicious dinner

Something more…Baby Addy took her first steps across the living room floor!

SAMPLE 2

Most mornings, you like to go for a run, eat a banana and then shower. Here's what that 5x2 would look like.

I saw…the sunrise

I heard…my running playlist

I smelled...the ocean

I tasted...my banana

I felt...my favorite running shirt

Today's goal is to...meal plan tonight for the week

You want your new night routine to be meditating for five minutes with a candle burning.

Sample

Tonight

I saw...my candle

I heard...my breath

I smelled...lavender (from my candle)

I tasted...water (after)

I felt...my yoga mat

I am grateful for...taking some time for myself

Something more...had some really good fish tacos for lunch

SAMPLE 3

You need to get straight to work in the morning. You can set a routine in your car that still brings you joy. Maybe it's a simple as listening to a podcast and drinking your favorite tea on your commute.

This morning

I saw...my to-go mug

I heard... *This American Life* podcast

I smelled...the spices in my tea

I tasted...the chai in my tea

I felt...my warm mug

Today's goal is to...go to yoga

Your night routine includes making breakfast for the next morning while listening to music.

<u>Sample</u>

Tonight

I saw...my mason jars

I heard...Pandora's 90s playlist

I smelled...the cinnamon for my overnight oats

I tasted...water

I felt...my socks

I am grateful for...not getting the sickness going around the office
Something more...

(Remember, you don't need to fill in this section)

SENSES CATEGORIES

In here you can add all the different things that fall into each category that create a positive feedback loop for you. I have filled in one row as example.

Taste	Touch	Smell	See	Hear
Coffee	Slippers	Coffee Beans	Ocean	Music

Practice Pages- Now it's your turn-

Think about your day and what you think you could easily start with as a 5x2. Write two versions down to get you started.

Your First 5x2

This morning

I saw... _____

I heard... _____

I smelled... _____

I tasted..._____

I felt..._____

Today's goal is to... _____

_____

Tonight

I saw... _____

I heard..._____

I smelled... _____

I tasted..._____

I felt... _____

I am grateful for... _____

Something more... _____

<u>Your Second 5x2</u>

This morning

I saw… _____

I heard… _____

I smelled… _____

I tasted… _____

I felt… _____

Today's goal is to… _____

_____

Tonight

I saw… _____

I heard… _____

I smelled… _____

I tasted… _____

I felt… _____

I am grateful for… _____

Something more… _____

_____

_____

My 5x2 Method Journal

This morning

I saw… _____

I heard … _____

I smelled… _____

I tasted…_____

I felt…_____

Today's goal is to… _____

_____

Tonight

I saw… _____

I heard…._____

I smelled…. _____

I tasted…_____

I felt… _____

I am grateful for … _____

Something more… _____

_____

_____

My 5x2 Method Journal

This morning

I saw… _____

I heard … _____

I smelled… _____

I tasted…_____

I felt…_____

Today's goal is to… _____

_____

Tonight

I saw… _____

I heard…._____

I smelled…. _____

I tasted…_____

I felt… _____

I am grateful for … _____

Something more… _____

_____

_____

My 5x2 Method Journal

This morning

I saw… _____

I heard … _____

I smelled… _____

I tasted…_____

I felt…_____

Today's goal is to… _____

_____

Tonight

I saw… _____

I heard…._____

I smelled…. _____

I tasted…_____

I felt… _____

I am grateful for … _____

Something more… _____

_____

_____

My 5x2 Method Journal

This morning

I saw… _____

I heard … _____

I smelled… _____

I tasted… _____

I felt… _____

Today's goal is to… _____

_____

Tonight

I saw… _____

I heard…. _____

I smelled…. _____

I tasted… _____

I felt… _____

I am grateful for … _____

Something more… _____

_____

_____

My 5x2 Method Journal

This morning

I saw… _____

I heard … _____

I smelled… _____

I tasted… _____

I felt… _____

Today's goal is to… _____

_____

Tonight

I saw… _____

I heard…. _____

I smelled…. _____

I tasted… _____

I felt… _____

I am grateful for … _____

Something more… _____

_____

_____

My 5x2 Method Journal

This morning

I saw… _____

I heard … _____

I smelled… _____

I tasted…_____

I felt…_____

Today's goal is to… _____

_____

Tonight

I saw… _____

I heard…._____

I smelled…. _____

I tasted…_____

I felt… _____

I am grateful for … _____

Something more… _____

_____

_____

My 5x2 Method Journal

This morning

I saw... _____

I heard ... _____

I smelled... _____

I tasted... _____

I felt... _____

Today's goal is to... _____

_____

Tonight

I saw... _____

I heard.... _____

I smelled.... _____

I tasted... _____

I felt... _____

I am grateful for ... _____

Something more... _____

_____

_____

My 5x2 Method Journal

This morning

I saw… _____

I heard … _____

I smelled… _____

I tasted…_____

I felt…_____

Today's goal is to… _____

_____

Tonight

I saw… _____

I heard…._____

I smelled…. _____

I tasted…_____

I felt… _____

I am grateful for … _____

Something more… _____

_____

_____

My 5x2 Method Journal

This morning

I saw… _____

I heard… _____

I smelled… _____

I tasted… _____

I felt… _____

Today's goal is to… _____

_____

Tonight

I saw… _____

I heard… _____

I smelled…. _____

I tasted… _____

I felt… _____

I am grateful for… _____

Something more… _____

_____

_____

FINAL THOUGHTS

"Do the best you can until you know better.
Then when you know better, do better."
-Maya Angelou-

I truly hope you've enjoyed our journey together. I greatly appreciate your interest and attention. One thing this book has certainly done for me is act as a constant reminder of the importance of self-awareness. Understanding and remembering the details of who you are and where you've been can add so much value to helping you get to where you want to go through this simple technique.

Consuming new concepts is always exciting at first, but they can often be easily forgotten. I've given you 7 pages of practice as a way to ingrain The 5x2 Method into your new routine.

I now want you to kick off the training wheels and use the skills that you've just developed to take control of your own happiness every single day. You can use the journal pages as a guide to refer back to if you get lost, just like having to call a coach for reminders every now and then.

But trust in yourself that you now possess the knowledge and strength of what you need to do to create a shift if at any time you feel out of alignment.

I wish you all the happiness that you deserve.

Chris DiVecchio

Chris DiVecchio

I don't want a
perfect life,
I want a happy life.

🙂

References:

1 Mathôt, S. & Van der Stigchel, S. (2015). New light on the mind's eye: the pupillary light response as active vision. *Current Directions in Psychological Science, 24,* 374-378.

2. The Hear The World Foundation

ABOUT THE AUTHOR

Chris DiVecchio is the Founder & Trainer of Premier, Mind & Body Health and Fitness in Los Angeles, California.

Chris brings a wealth of self-development transformation mixed with a very practical technique to his fitness training. Coming from a bodybuilding background and a D1 collegiate hockey career, Chris realized that he wanted to teach his simple techniques and strategies to help others achieve both physical and mental acuity.

As a fitness trainer and lifestyle specialist, Chris has a knack for inspiring accountability and achieving results quickly. With each client, Chris develops a unique and effective nutrition and personal training strategy. His vast knowledge of great recipes and food combinations allow him to create a diet that not only tastes great but will also be easy to maintain.

Chris has developed innovative fitness concepts and practices for all types of clients who are all working through very different life experiences.

Chris's combination of inner and outer work is what inspired him to come up with The 5x2 Method, as overall wellbeing is more than just physical.

He believes everyone is just trying to live the best life they can and be the best version of themselves.
Want to get in touch with Chris?

Website   www.pmblife.com
Email   Chris@pmblife.com
Facebook   fb.com/PMBLife
Instagram instagram.com/ChrisDiVecchio
Twitter   twitter.com/PremierMindBody

Made in the USA
San Bernardino, CA
12 May 2018